MASTERING THE MODERN MARKETPLACE: 10 STRATEGIES FOR THRIVING AS A SMALL BUSINESS IN 2024 (AND BEYOND)

Chapter 1: The Evolving Landscape - Understanding the Challenges and Opportunities

- ☐ The Rise of the Digital Economy
- ☐ The Changing Consumer Landscape
- ☐ Identifying Market Trends and Opportunities
- ☐ The Impact of Technology on Small Business

Chapter 2: Building a Strong Foundation - Defining Your Vision and Mission

- ☐ Crafting a Compelling Mission Statement
- ☐ Identifying Your Core Values
- ☐ Defining Your Target Audience
- ☐ Understanding Your Unique Selling Proposition (USP)

Chapter 3: The Power of Digital Marketing - Reaching Your Audience in the Age of Information

- ☐ Optimizing Your Website for Search Engines (SEO)
- ☐ Mastering Content Marketing Strategies
- ☐ Harnessing the Power of Social Media Marketing
- ☐ Exploring Paid Advertising Options
- ☐ Building an Email Marketing Strategy

Chapter 4: Building Trust and Credibility - The Power of Social Proof and Customer Experience

- ☐ The Importance of Customer Reviews and Testimonials
- ☐ Cultivating Customer Loyalty
- ☐ Delivering Exceptional Customer Service Interactions
- ☐ The Value of Transparency and Authenticity
- ☐ Building a Positive Online Reputation

Chapter 5: Embracing Innovation - Emerging Technologies and Tools for Small Businesses

- ☐ The Rise of Generative AI and Content Creation
- ☐ Utilizing Cloud-Based Solutions for Streamlining Operations
- ☐ Leveraging Data Analytic and Business Intelligence
- ☐ Exploring Automation Platforms for Increased Efficiency

Chapter 6: Building a Strong Brand Identity - Standing Out in a Crowded Marketplace

- ☐ Unearthing Your Brand's Essence - Mission, Values, Personality
- ☐ Understanding Your Target Audience - Needs, Pain Points, Aspirations
- ☐ Crafting a Compelling Brand Narrative
- ☐ Integrating Your Story into Everything You Do
- ☐ Maintaining Brand Consistency Across Platforms

Chapter 7: The Power of Storytelling - Captivating Your Audience in a Noisy World

Mastering the Modern Marketplace: 10 Strategies for Thriving as a Small Business in 2024 (and Beyond)

Introduction: The Evolving Landscape of Small Business

The world of small business is constantly evolving. Gone are the days of relying solely on brick-and-mortar storefronts and traditional advertising. Today's successful entrepreneurs need to be digital natives, keenly aware of the ever-changing customer landscape. This ebook will equip you with the knowledge and strategies to navigate this dynamic environment and thrive as a small business owner.

- Why Stories Matter: The Science Behind the Captivation
- The Anatomy of a Compelling Story - The Hero's Journey
- Storytelling Formats: Choosing the Right Medium for Your Message
- Weaving Your Brand Story into the Fabric of Your Business

Chapter 8: Mastering the Evolving Payment Landscape - Embracing New Technologies for Seamless Transactions

- The Rise of Mobile Wallets and Contactless Payments
- Understanding Buy Now, Pay Later (BNPL) Options
- Choosing the Right Payment Mix for Your Business
- Integrating New Payment Technologies - Actionable Steps
- Staying Informed About Payment Security Trends

Chapter 9: Cultivating a Sustainable Future - Eco-Conscious Practices for Your Business

- The Importance of Sustainability in Today's Business Environment
- Implementing Sustainable Practices in Your Operations
- Eco-Conscious Marketing Strategies and Messaging
- Building a Socially Responsible Brand Reputation

Chapter 10: The Future is Now - Embracing Continuous Learning and Innovation

- Lifelong Learning as the Fuel for Growth
- Strategies for Continuous Learning and Development
- Igniting the Spark of Innovation in Your Organization
- The Importance of Celebrating Innovation and New Ideas
- Conclusion: The Journey to Success is Continuous

CHAPTER 1: THE POWER OF DIGITAL MARKETING - REACHING YOUR AUDIENCE IN THE AGE OF INFORMATION

In today's hyper-connected world, traditional marketing methods are no longer enough. Gone are the days of relying solely on flyers and newspaper ads to reach your target audience. The modern customer journey begins online, and for small businesses, having a robust digital marketing strategy is no longer optional; it's essential. This chapter will delve into the key digital marketing tactics you can leverage to reach your audience, build brand awareness, and drive sales.

CONTENT IS KING (AND QUEEN):

The cornerstone of any successful digital marketing strategy is high-quality content. Creating valuable and informative content establishes your brand as an authority in your niche, builds trust with potential customers, and attracts organic traffic to your website or social media channels. Think of content as a conversation starter.

Blog Posts:
Share your expertise by writing informative blog posts that address your target audience's pain points and interests.

Infographics: These visually appealing explainers can condense complex information into easily digestible content perfect for social media sharing.

Videos: Harness the power of video marketing to showcase your products or services, offer tutorials, or share customer testimonials.

SEO: The Key to Organic Visibility: Search Engine Optimization (SEO) is optimizing your website and content to rank higher in search engine results pages (SERPs) for relevant keywords. The higher your ranking, the more likely potential customers will discover your business when searching online.

HERE ARE SOME ESSENTIAL SEO TACTICS TO CONSIDER:

Keyword Research: Identify the keywords your target audience is searching for and incorporate them naturally into your content.

Website Optimization: Ensure your website has a clean design, fast loading speed, and is mobile-friendly.

Backlinks: Encourage other websites to link to yours, which signals authority to search engines.

Social Media Mastery: Building Your Online Community: Social media platforms offer a powerful way to connect with your target audience, build brand awareness, and foster community. The key is to identify the platforms where your audience spends their time, be it Facebook, Instagram, TikTok, or a niche-specific platform.

Once you've identified your platform(s) of choice, Develop a Consistent Brand Voice. Establish a distinct personality that reflects your brand values and resonates with your audience.
Visual Storytelling: People are drawn to visually appealing content. Use high-quality images and videos to grab attention and tell your brand story.

Embrace Engagement Features: Don't just broadcast messages. Utilize interactive features like polls, quizzes, and live videos to engage your audience and build a two-way conversation.

The Rise of Short-Form Video Content:

Platforms like TikTok and Instagram Reels have revolutionized the way we consume content. These short-form video formats offer a dynamic way to connect with potential customers in a fun and engaging way.

HERE ARE SOME IDEAS FOR CREATING BITE-SIZED VIDEO CONTENT:

Product Demonstrations: Showcase your products or services in action.

Behind-the-Scenes Glimpses: Offer viewers a peek into your company culture and humanize your brand.

User-Generated Content (UGC): Encourage customers to share their experiences with your brand using a specific hashtag and feature their content on your channels.

By embracing these digital marketing techniques, you can effectively reach your target audience in the age of information, build stronger brand relationships, and ultimately drive sales for your small business.

CHAPTER 2: LEVERAGING SOCIAL PROOF AND INFLUENCER MARKETING – BUILDING TRUST IN A DIGITAL WORLD

In today's digital landscape, trust is paramount. With countless businesses vying for attention online, potential customers are increasingly cautious before purchasing. This chapter explores two powerful tools for building trust and credibility: social proof and influencer marketing.

The Power of Us: Harnessing User-Generated Content (UGC)

Imagine a potential customer considering your product. They've seen your website and social media posts, but they're still hesitant. Suddenly, they come across a glowing review from a satisfied customer or an Instagram photo showcasing your product in action. This, my friend, is the magic of User-Generated Content (UGC).

UGC leverages the power of authenticity. Real people sharing their positive experiences with your brand builds social proof and fosters trust with potential customers. Here's how to tap into the power of UGC:

Run UGC Campaigns: Encourage customers to share their experiences with your brand using a specific hashtag. You can offer incentives like discounts or product giveaways to participate.
Showcase UGC Across Your Channels: Feature positive reviews, testimonials, and photos on your website, social media platforms, and email marketing campaigns.
Respond and Engage: Show your appreciation for UGC by responding to comments and messages. This fosters a sense of community and encourages further engagement.

The Rise of the Micro-Influencer: Building Authentic Relationships
Influencer marketing has become a cornerstone of many digital marketing strategies. However, the days of solely chasing celebrity endorsements are gone. Today, the focus is on micro-influencers. These individuals have a dedicated, engaged following within a specific niche, often aligned with your target audience.

Here's why partnering with micro-influencers can be a winning strategy:

Authenticity: Micro-influencers are known for their genuine connections with their followers. Their recommendations hold more weight and feel less like a forced advertisement.
Targeted Reach: By partnering with micro-influencers in your niche, you can reach a highly relevant audience interested in products or services like yours.
Cost-Effective: Collaborations with micro-influencers are often more affordable than celebrity endorsements, making them an excellent option for small businesses.

Building Successful Influencer Partnerships:

Identify the Right Partners: Don't just focus on follower count. Look for micro-influencers whose brand values and audience align with yours.

Develop Authentic Collaborations: Don't dictate scripts or force robotic endorsements. Please work with the influencer to create natural content that resonates with their audience.

Track and Measure Results: Use analytics tools to track the reach and engagement generated by influencer campaigns. This allows you to refine your strategy for future collaborations.

By leveraging the power of social proof and influencer marketing, you can build trust with potential customers, increase brand awareness, and ultimately drive sales for your small business. Remember, authenticity is critical. When customers feel a genuine connection to your brand and the people who represent it, they're more likely to become loyal advocates.

CHAPTER 3: THRIVING IN THE NEW LANDSCAPE: ADAPTING TO THE MODERN WORKFORCE

The landscape of work is undergoing a significant shift. Gone are the days of a one-size-fits-all approach to employee management. Today's workforce, particularly millennials and Gen Z, prioritize flexibility, work-life balance, and a sense of purpose in their careers. As a small business owner, adapting to these evolving preferences is crucial for attracting and retaining top talent. This chapter explores two key areas: the rise of remote work and prioritizing employee wellbeing.

THE REMOTE REVOLUTION: EMBRACING THE WORK-FROM-ANYWHERE MODEL

The COVID-19 pandemic accelerated a trend already gaining momentum – remote work. Many employees have discovered the benefits of working outside a traditional office setting, enjoying greater flexibility and improved work-life balance. For small businesses, offering remote work options can be a win-win situation.

HERE'S HOW TO EMBRACE THE REMOTE WORK REVOLUTION:

Identify Suitable Roles: Not all positions are well-suited for a remote environment. Analyze your current roles and identify those that can be effectively performed remotely.

Invest in the Right Tools: Equip your remote team with the necessary tools for communication and collaboration. This could include project management platforms, video conferencing software, and secure cloud storage solutions.

Establish Clear Communication Channels: Distance shouldn't hinder communication. Set clear expectations, define communication protocols, and encourage regular check-ins with your remote team.

PRIORITIZING EMPLOYEE WELLBEING: INVESTING IN YOUR PEOPLE

In today's competitive job market, creating a positive work environment that prioritizes employee wellbeing is no longer a perk; it's a necessity. Employees who feel valued, supported, and empowered are more productive and likely to stay with your company.

HERE ARE SOME WAYS TO PRIORITIZE EMPLOYEE WELLBEING:

Flexible Work Arrangements: Offer flexible work schedules, remote work options, or compressed workweeks to accommodate individual needs and promote work-life balance.

Invest in Training and Development: Employees with growth and skill development opportunities are more engaged and satisfied. Provide training programs, mentorship opportunities, and support for professional development.

Foster a Culture of Open Communication: Create an environment where employees feel comfortable voicing their concerns and offering suggestions. Regular team meetings, anonymous feedback surveys, and open-door policies foster a sense of trust and transparency.

By adapting to the modern workforce's evolving needs and prioritizing employee wellbeing, you can build a loyal and high-performing team—a crucial asset for any small business looking to thrive in the ever-changing marketplace. Happy employees are productive, and a positive work environment is an investment in your business's future success.

CHAPTER 4: THE SUSTAINABLE SHIFT - EMBRACING ECO-CONSCIOUS PRACTICES

In today's environmentally conscious world, consumers are increasingly making purchasing decisions based on a company's commitment to sustainability. This isn't just a passing trend – it's a fundamental shift in consumer behavior that small businesses can't afford to ignore. This chapter explores the growing importance of sustainability in the marketplace and provides actionable advice on integrating eco-conscious practices into your small business operations.

THE GREEN REVOLUTION: WHY SUSTAINABILITY MATTERS

Sustainability refers to the ability to meet the needs of the present without compromising the ability of future generations to meet their own needs. In the context of business, it's about minimizing your environmental impact while ensuring the long-term viability of your company.

HERE'S WHY EMBRACING SUSTAINABILITY MATTERS FOR YOUR SMALL BUSINESS:

Meeting Customer Demand: A growing number of consumers prioritize eco-friendly products and services. Studies show they're willing to pay a premium for sustainable options and support businesses aligning with their values.

Enhanced Brand Reputation: Demonstrating a commitment to sustainability can significantly enhance your brand reputation. Eco-conscious practices position you as a responsible and forward-thinking company, attracting potential partners and environmentally-conscious customers.

Reduced Costs and Increased Efficiency: Sustainable practices often lead to cost savings. This could involve reducing energy consumption, minimizing waste, or utilizing recycled materials. By operating more efficiently, you can improve your bottom line.

Future-Proofing Your Business: Environmental regulations constantly evolve, and sustainable practices can help ensure your business remains compliant. By being proactive, you can avoid potential disruptions and fines in the future.

Walking the Walk: Implementing Sustainable Practices

So, you're convinced of the importance of sustainability. Now what? Here are some practical steps you can take to integrate eco-conscious practices into your small business:

Product and Service Offerings:

Sustainable Products: Source and sell products made from recycled or eco-friendly materials. This could include anything from organic clothing to biodegradable packaging materials.

Durable and Long-Lasting: Focus on offering high-quality, durable products built to last. This reduces the need for frequent replacements and minimizes waste.

Sustainable Services: Consider how you can offer services that promote sustainability. For example, a cleaning company could use eco-friendly cleaning products, or a landscaping company could specialize in native plant installation.

Supply Chain and Operations:

Sustainable Sourcing: Partner with suppliers who share your commitment to sustainability. Look for companies that use eco-friendly practices and prioritize ethical sourcing.

Reduce, Reuse, Recycle: Implement a waste reduction strategy in your workplace. This could involve minimizing packaging materials, offering recycling options for employees, and reusing office supplies whenever possible.

Energy Efficiency: Audit your energy consumption and identify areas for improvement. Invest in energy-efficient appliances, lighting systems, and HVAC equipment. If feasible, consider utilizing clean energy sources like solar power.

Minimize Transportation Emissions: Encourage employees to utilize public transportation, carpool, or cycle to work whenever possible. If you have a delivery fleet, explore options for electric vehicles or route optimization to reduce fuel consumption.

Marketing and Communication:
Transparency is Key: Don't greenwash – making unsubstantiated claims about your sustainability efforts. Be transparent about your initiatives and communicate your commitment to eco-conscious practices.

Storytelling and Education: Use your marketing platforms to educate consumers about your sustainability efforts. Share stories about your eco-friendly suppliers, the sustainable materials used in your products, or your community involvement in environmental projects.

Partner with Eco-Conscious Organizations: Collaborate with environmental organizations or participate in green initiatives in your community. This demonstrates your commitment to sustainability and allows you to reach a wider audience of environmentally conscious consumers.

Challenges and Overcoming Obstacles
Transitioning to a more sustainable business model will take time. Here are some common challenges you might encounter and how to overcome them:

Cost Concerns: Sustainable practices may require an initial investment in new equipment, materials, or processes. However, remember that these investments can often lead to cost savings in the long run through reduced energy consumption and waste minimization.

Limited Knowledge: Feeling overwhelmed? Feel free to seek out resources and information. Numerous organizations offer guidance on implementing sustainable business practices. Industry associations, government agencies, and environmental NGOs can be valuable sources of knowledge and support.

Consumer Skepticism: Greenwashing is a real issue, and some consumers may be skeptical about your sustainability claims.

Focus on transparency and authenticity. Back up your claims with data and actions, and build trust by consistently demonstrating your commitment to

CHAPTER 5: EMBRACING INNOVATION - EMERGING TECHNOLOGIES AND TOOLS FOR SMALL BUSINESSES

The business landscape is constantly evolving, driven by technological advancements. As a small business owner, staying ahead of the curve and embracing new tools can give you a significant competitive advantage. This chapter explores some of the most promising emerging technologies and how you can leverage them to streamline operations, enhance marketing efforts, and ultimately achieve your business goals.

THE RISE OF THE MACHINES (BUT NOT QUITE): GENERATIVE AI AND CONTENT CREATION

Artificial intelligence (AI) is no longer the stuff of science fiction. Today, a specific branch of AI, generative AI, is transforming how businesses approach content creation. Generative AI utilizes machine learning algorithms to create new content, such as text, images, or music. While AI will only partially replace human creativity, it can be a powerful tool for small businesses struggling to keep up with the constant demand for fresh content.

Here are some ways you can leverage generative AI:

Content Brainstorming: Are you stuck for blog post ideas or social media captions? Generative AI tools can help you brainstorm new ideas and overcome writer's block.

Generating Product Descriptions: Optimize your website with engaging and informative product descriptions. AI tools can help you create clear, concise copy highlighting product features and benefits.

Social Media Management: Are you struggling to maintain a consistent social media presence? Generative AI can help you craft engaging captions and headlines for social media posts.

Remember: AI is a tool, not a replacement for human creativity. Always edit AI-generated content for accuracy and brand voice, and ensure it resonates with your target audience.

Beyond Content: Other Innovative Tools for Small Businesses: The world of technology offers many tools and platforms specifically designed to empower small businesses. Here are a few examples to consider:

Cloud-Based Solutions: Embrace the flexibility and scalability of cloud-based solutions. Cloud storage allows you to access your data from anywhere, while cloud-based applications offer features like project management, accounting, and customer relationship management (CRM).

Data Analytics and Business Intelligence: Data is king in today's business world. Utilize analytics tools to gain deeper insights into your customer behavior, website traffic, and marketing campaigns. Use these insights to optimize your offerings and effectively target your marketing efforts.

Automation Platforms: Automate repetitive tasks to free up your time and resources for more strategic endeavors. Tools can automate tasks like email marketing, social media scheduling, and data entry, allowing you to focus on higher-level business development.

STAYING INFORMED: A CULTURE OF CONTINUOUS LEARNING

Technology is constantly evolving, so staying informed is crucial. Here are some ways to ensure you're up-to-date on the latest trends and tools:

Industry Publications and Blogs: Subscribe to industry publications and blogs to stay abreast of the latest technological advancements relevant to your niche.

Attend Conferences and Webinars: Many conferences and webinars focus on emerging technologies for small businesses. Attending these events can be valuable for learning about new tools and networking with other entrepreneurs.

Experiment and Embrace a Growth Mindset: Be bold and experiment with new technologies. Start small, try different tools, and see what works best for your business. Embrace a culture of continuous learning and stay curious about the possibilities technology can offer.

By embracing innovation and utilizing the latest tools, you can streamline your operations, enhance your marketing efforts, and gain a competitive edge in the ever-changing business landscape. Remember, technology is meant to empower you, not replace you. Use it strategically to free up your time for creative thinking, strategic planning, and building meaningful customer connections.

CHAPTER 6: BUILDING A STRONG BRAND IDENTITY - STANDING OUT IN A CROWDED MARKETPLACE

In today's saturated markets, more than simply having a great product or service is needed. What truly sets successful brands apart is a strong brand identity. This identity is the foundation of how your audience perceives you, encompassing your values, mission, and the unique personality that breathes life into your business.

This chapter explores the power of crafting a compelling brand story—a narrative that goes beyond product features and speaks directly to your target audience. A well-told brand story fosters connection, builds trust, and positions your brand for long-term success.

MASTERING THE MODERN MARKETPLACE: 10 STRATEGIES FOR THRIVING A...

UNEARTHING YOUR BRAND'S ESSENCE

The journey to a powerful brand story starts with introspection. Here's where you get to know yourself, your brand, and what makes it tick:

Mission & Values: What is your brand's core purpose? What fundamental beliefs guide your operations?

Unique Selling Proposition (USP): Why are you different? What makes your brand the obvious choice over competitors?

Brand Personality: Imagine your brand as a character. What personality traits would it possess? Would it be trustworthy, innovative, or playful?

Understanding Your Audience: The Missing Piece: An exceptional brand story isn't a monologue – it's a conversation. To craft a narrative that resonates, you need to understand your target audience:

Target Market: Who are you trying to reach with your message?
Needs & Pain Points: What challenges do your ideal customers face? How can your brand alleviate them?

Values & Aspirations: What motivates your audience? What kind of lifestyle do they strive for?
By understanding your audience's emotional landscape, you can tailor a story that speaks directly to their desires and aspirations.

Crafting Your Brand Narrative: A Guide:-Now comes the exciting part – weaving your brand's essence and audience insights into a captivating story:

Storytelling Framework: Consider established storytelling structures like the Hero's Journey to build a framework for your narrative.

Emotional Connection: Stories that tap into emotions leave a lasting impression.

Conflict & Resolution: Showcase how your brand empowers your audience to overcome challenges.

Authenticity is Key: Let your brand's genuine voice shine through in your narrative.

Weaving Your Story into the Fabric of Your Brand. A brand story isn't a one-time event; it's an ongoing thread woven into every aspect of your business:

Brand Story in Everything: Integrate your brand story into marketing materials, customer interactions, and product packaging.

Consistency is Key: Ensure your brand story resonates consistently across all platforms, online and offline.

MAYORADEY

REFINING YOUR STORY FOR LASTING IMPACT

The best brand stories are living entities that evolve with your business:

Seek Feedback: Get input on your brand story from your target audience and refine it based on their insights.

Test & Adapt: Be prepared to adapt your story as your brand grows and the market landscape shifts.
Following these steps, you can craft a brand story that stands out, fosters connections with your audience, and propels your brand toward long-term success. Remember, your brand story is a powerful tool – use it wisely to carve out your unique space in a crowded marketplace.

CHAPTER 7: DATA-DRIVEN DECISIONS - MEASURING YOUR SUCCESS

In today's dynamic business environment, more than intuition and guesswork is needed. Data-driven decision-making is paramount to navigating the market's ever-changing tides and achieving sustainable growth. This chapter delves into the power of data analytics, equipping you with the tools and strategies to objectively measure your success and make informed choices that propel your brand forward.

WHY EMBRACE DATA-DRIVEN DECISIONS?

Imagine steering a ship blindfolded – that's essentially what running a business is like without data. Data is your compass, providing valuable insights into customer behavior, campaign effectiveness, and overall brand performance. By leveraging analytics, you can:

Gain a Clearer Picture: Data paints a detailed picture of your target audience, their preferences, and their interactions with your brand.

Optimize Your Efforts: Identify what's working well in your marketing campaigns and double down on those strategies. Conversely, data can pinpoint areas for improvement, allowing you to refine your approach and allocate resources more effectively.

Make Informed Decisions: Data empowers you to move beyond assumptions and base your choices on concrete evidence. This leads to more strategic decision-making across all aspects of your business.

Measure ROI: Track your marketing campaign's return on investment (ROI). This will allow you to demonstrate the value you're generating and optimize your spending for maximum impact.

Stay Agile: The business landscape is constantly evolving. Data analytics provides real-time insights that enable you to adapt your strategies quickly and effectively to changing trends and customer needs.

Data-driven decision-making isn't just a trend; it's a fundamental shift in how successful businesses operate. Here's a look at ten essential pieces of advice to get you started on your data-driven journey:

1. Define Your Goals & Objectives:

The foundation of any data analysis effort is a clear understanding of what you're trying to achieve. Start by outlining your specific goals and objectives. Are you aiming to increase website traffic, boost brand awareness, or drive conversions? Clearly defined goals will guide you in selecting the right metrics to track and analyze.

2. Identify Key Performance Indicators (KPIs):

KPIs are quantifiable metrics that act as benchmarks for measuring progress toward achieving goals. Business KPIs include website traffic, conversion rates, social media engagement, customer acquisition costs (CAC), and lifetime value (CLTV). Selecting the right KPIs depends on your specific goals and industry.

3. Leverage Analytic Tools:
Fortunately, you can be something other than a data scientist to leverage the power of analytics. Today, many user-friendly tools are available to help you track and analyze data. Popular options include Google Analytics, Facebook Insights, and social media management platforms that offer built-in analytics dashboards. Many marketing automation platforms also provide comprehensive analytics capabilities.

CHAPTER 8: THE POWER OF STORYTELLING - CAPTIVATING YOUR AUDIENCE IN A NOISY WORLD

In today's digital age, consumers are bombarded with information from all sides. Attention spans are shrinking, and the competition for eyeballs is fierce. So, how do you cut through the noise and make your small business stand out? The answer lies in the age-old art of storytelling.

This chapter explores the power of storytelling as a marketing tool. You'll learn how to craft compelling narratives that connect with your audience on an emotional level, build trust, and ultimately drive sales. We'll explore different storytelling techniques, explore content formats that resonate, and provide practical tips for weaving your brand story into every aspect of your marketing strategy.

WHY STORIES MATTER: THE SCIENCE BEHIND THE CAPTIVATION

Stories aren't just whimsical tales—they profoundly impact the human brain. Studies show that stories activate different brain parts associated with emotion, memory, and decision-making. When we listen to a story, we subconsciously put ourselves in the characters' shoes, experiencing their joys and sorrows as if they were our own. This emotional connection is what makes stories so powerful and persuasive.

Here's a breakdown of the science behind storytelling's effectiveness:

Emotional Connection: Stories trigger the release of oxytocin, a hormone associated with empathy and trust. When we connect with characters on an emotional level, we're more likely to trust the brand they represent.

Enhanced Memory: Stories are easier to remember than dry facts and figures. Our brains are wired to process narratives, making stories more effective for communicating information and brand messages.

Influencing Decisions: Stories can subtly influence our decision-making processes. You can subtly nudge your audience towards purchasing by showcasing how your product or service helps the protagonist overcome a challenge.

THE ANATOMY OF A COMPELLING STORY: CRAFTING YOUR NARRATIVE ARC

Not all stories are created equal. To truly captivate your audience, you must craft a narrative that follows a clear structure and evokes emotions. Here are some key elements to consider when building your brand story:

The Hero's Journey: This classic storytelling framework is robust for structuring your brand narrative. It follows a protagonist's journey who faces challenges, experiences growth, and ultimately emerges victorious.

Identifying Your Hero: In your brand story, the hero is your ideal customer. What challenges do they face? What are their desires and aspirations?

The Obstacle: What stands in the way of your hero achieving their goals? This could be a specific problem your product solves, or a general pain points your target audience experiences.

The Guide: This is where your brand comes in! You are the wise mentor who equips the hero with the knowledge and tools (your product or service) to overcome the obstacle.

The Resolution: Showcase how your product or service helps your hero achieve their goals and live a happier, more fulfilling life.

STORYTELLING FORMATS: CHOOSING THE RIGHT MEDIUM FOR YOUR MESSAGE

Now that you understand the core elements of a compelling story, it's time to choose the correct format to deliver your message. Here are some popular storytelling formats for small businesses:

Blog Posts: Share informative and engaging blog posts that tell stories about your brand, customers, or the challenges your products solve.

Customer Testimonials: Feature stories from satisfied customers who have benefited from your products or services. Real-life stories add a robust layer of authenticity and credibility.

Video Marketing: Compelling video stories can showcase your brand personality, product demonstrations, or behind-the-scenes glimpses into your company culture.

Social Media Stories: Utilize the ephemeral storytelling features of platforms like Instagram and Facebook to capture fleeting moments and connect with your audience casually and engagingly.
Case Studies: In-depth case studies can showcase your product or service's transformative impact on real businesses.

Podcasts: Interview industry experts, share customer success stories, or even create a narrative podcast series that weaves your brand story into a fictional narrative.

Weaving Your Brand Story into the Fabric of Your Business

Your brand story shouldn't be confined to a single blog post or marketing campaign. It should be the guiding light that permeates every aspect of your business. Here's how to integrate storytelling into your brand identity:

Mission Statement: Create a mission statement encapsulating your brand story and core values.
Website Content: Let your brand story shine through your website copy, product descriptions, and "About Us" section.

Customer Service Interactions: Train your customer service team to deliver exceptional service that reflects your brand personality and story.

Packaging Design: Your product packaging can be a powerful storytelling tool. Consider incorporating elements of your brand narrative into the design.

MAYORADEY

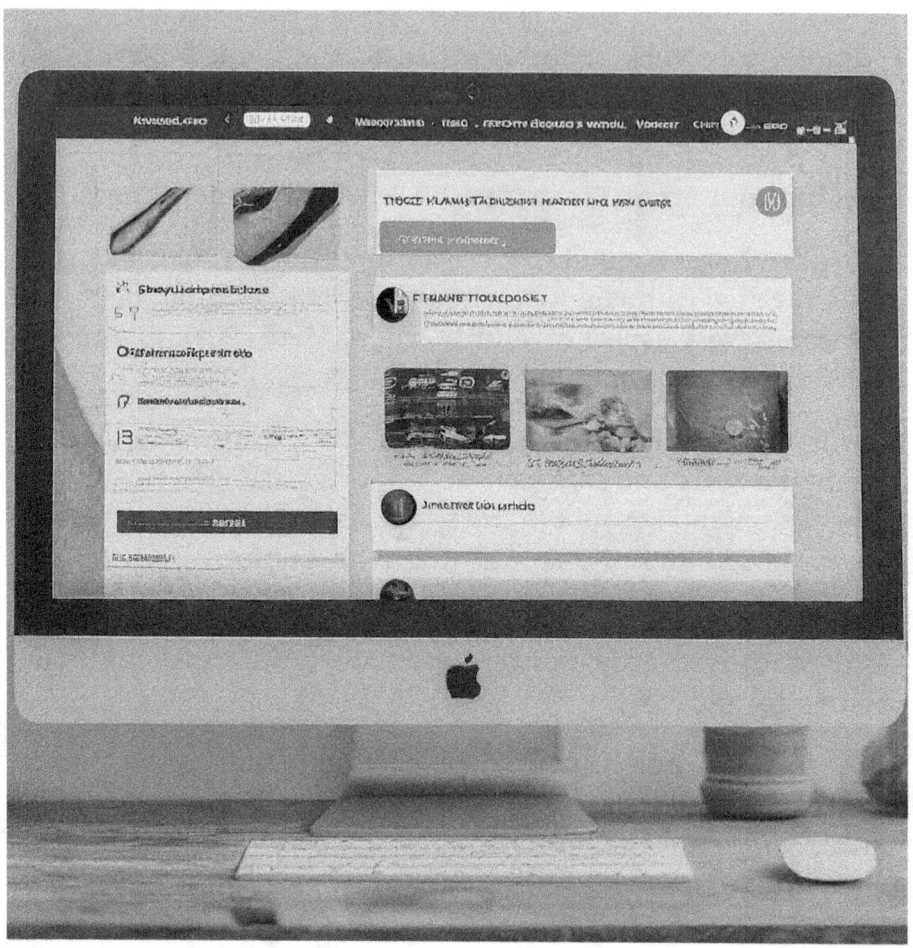

CHAPTER 9: MASTERING THE EVOLVING PAYMENT LANDSCAPE - EMBRACING NEW TECHNOLOGIES FOR SEAMLESS TRANSACTIONS

The way we pay for goods and services is undergoing a dramatic transformation. Cash is slowly fading into the background, and a new era of digital wallets, contactless payments, and alternative payment methods is upon us. Navigating this evolving landscape can take time and effort for small business owners. However, embracing these new technologies can unlock significant benefits —improved customer experience, increased efficiency, and potential security advantages.

This chapter equips you with the knowledge and actionable steps to stay ahead of the curve in the world of payments. We'll explore the latest trends, delve into the benefits and considerations of various payment options, and provide practical guidance on integrating these technologies into your business operations.

THE CHANGING FACE OF PAYMENTS: A GLIMPSE INTO THE FUTURE

Here are some key trends shaping the future of payments:

The Rise of Mobile Wallets: Mobile wallets like Apple Pay and Google Pay allow customers to store their payment information securely on their smartphones and make contactless payments at participating merchants. These solutions offer consumers a fast, convenient, and secure payment experience.

Contactless Payments: Contactless payment technology, such as chip-and-PIN cards and near-field communication (NFC), allows customers to tap or wave their cards or mobile devices at a reader to complete a transaction. This eliminates the need for physical card swipes, improving transaction speed and security.

Buy Now, Pay Later (BNPL) Options: BNPL services like Afterpay and Klarna are gaining traction. They allow customers to split their purchases into interest-free installments, which is an attractive option for budget-conscious consumers and can increase business sales.

The Cryptocurrency Conundrum: Cryptocurrencies like Bitcoin are a relatively new payment method with a volatile market. While not yet widely adopted for everyday transactions, some businesses are starting to accept them, catering to a tech-savvy customer segment.

UNDERSTANDING THE PAYMENT ECOSYSTEM: A BREAKDOWN OF KEY PLAYERS

To navigate the payment landscape effectively, it's essential to understand the different players involved:

Payment Processors: Companies like Stripe, PayPal, and Square act as intermediaries between merchants and banks, facilitating the authorization and settlement of electronic payments. They often offer additional services like fraud prevention and data security.

Payment Gateways: These secure platforms integrate with your website or point-of-sale (POS) system, allowing you to accept online and in-person payments. Choosing the right gateway is crucial for ensuring insurgence and protecting your business.

Merchant Accounts: A merchant account is a business bank account designed to receive customer payments. Payment processors typically require a merchant account to settle funds received through their platform.

CHOOSING THE RIGHT PAYMENT MIX FOR YOUR BUSINESS

There needs to be more than a one-size-fits-all solution for payment options. The best approach for your business depends on several factors, including:

Your Target Audience: Understanding your customer demographics and preferred payment methods is crucial. Tech-savvy millennials favor mobile wallets, while older generations prefer traditional credit cards.

Industry Standards: Certain industries have established payment norms. For example, contactless payments are becoming increasingly common in the restaurant industry.

Transaction Volume and Value: Consider your business's average transaction value and volume. Mobile wallets might be ideal for high-volume, low-value transactions, while credit cards might be more suitable for larger purchases.

ACTIONABLE STEPS: INTEGRATING NEW PAYMENT TECHNOLOGIES

Ready to embrace the future of payments? Here are some steps to take:

Evaluate Your Current Payment System: Analyze your existing payment processing setup and identify any areas for improvement.

Research New Payment Options: Explore the available payment solutions, considering factors like transaction fees, ease of integration, and security features.

Choose a Payment Processor and Gateway: Select a reputable payment processor and gateway that aligns with your business needs and budget. Many payment processors offer all-in-one solutions that combine processing and gateway services.

Integrate the Payment Gateway with Your POS System: Ensure smooth transaction processing by integrating your chosen payment gateway with your POS system or online shopping cart. Most payment processors provide detailed integration guides and support resources.

Educate Your Staff: Train your employees on the new payment methods and ensure they understand customer inquiries related to these options.

Communicate with Your Customers: Inform your customers about the new payment options you accept through your website, social media channels, and in-store signage. Offer clear instructions on how to use these methods.

Stay Informed: The payment landscape is constantly evolving. Stay up-to-date on the latest trends and security best practices to ensure your business remains competitive and secure.

CHAPTER 10: THE FUTURE IS NOW - EMBRACING CONTINUOUS LEARNING AND INNOVATION

Congratulations! You've reached the final chapter of this guide. Throughout this book, we've explored a range of powerful strategies to help your small business thrive in the ever-evolving modern marketplace. You've learned to leverage technology, craft a compelling brand story, and prioritize customer experience to achieve sustainable success.

However, the business landscape is dynamic, constantly shifting and adapting to new trends and technologies. The key to remaining competitive lies in embracing continuous learning and fostering a culture of innovation within your organization.

This chapter explores the importance of lifelong learning for small businesses and provides practical tips on staying informed and adapting to change. We'll also delve into the power of fostering innovation to unlock new opportunities and propel your business forward.

MAYORADEY

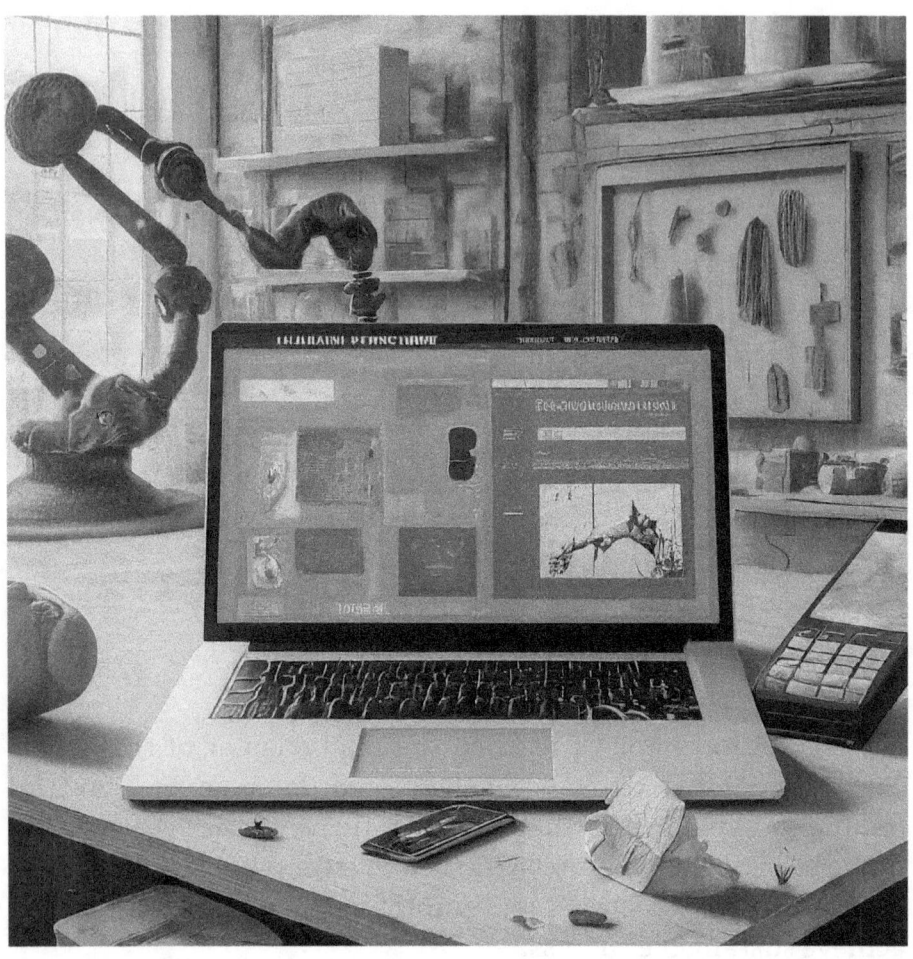

LIFELONG LEARNING: THE FUEL FOR GROWTH

In today's rapidly changing world, knowledge is not static; it's a continuous journey. Businesses that must adapt and embrace new ideas will stay caught up. Here's why lifelong learning is crucial for small businesses:

Staying Ahead of the Curve: New technologies, marketing trends, and customer preferences emerge constantly. Continuous learning ensures you stay informed and can leverage these advancements.

Identifying New Opportunities: By keeping your mind open to new ideas, you can locate potential market gaps and develop innovative products or services that cater to unmet customer needs.

Enhancing Your Skillset: Technology constantly evolves, and new marketing tools and platforms are introduced regularly. Investing in learning and development for your team allows everyone to stay up-to-date and perform at their best.

Fostering a Culture of Curiosity: A learning mindset encourages creativity, problem-solving, and critical thinking within your organization.

STRATEGIES FOR LIFELONG LEARNING:

Industry Publications and Blogs: Subscribe to relevant industry publications and blogs to stay informed about the latest trends in your niche 'stations—many offline or online content.

Podcasts and Audiobooks: Leverage your commute or downtime by listening to industry-related podcasts and audiobooks. This is a fantastic way to learn on the go.

Conferences and Webinars: Attend industry conferences and webinars to network with other professionals and learn from leading experts. Many events are now offered online, making them more accessible.

Online Courses and Training Programs: Invest in online courses and training programs to develop new skills or deepen your understanding of specific topics. There are numerous affordable and reputable platforms offering a wide range of courses.

Embrace Experimentation: Be bold and experiment with new ideas and approaches. Start small, track your results, and be prepared to pivot if necessary.

Igniting the Spark of Innovation: Innovation isn't just about developing revolutionary new products; it's about finding creative solutions to existing problems and improving operational efficiency. Here are ways to foster a culture of innovation:

Encourage Employee Ideas: Create an environment where employees feel comfortable sharing ideas and suggestions. Hold brainstorming sessions and reward innovative thinking.

Invest in Research and Development: Dedicate resources to research and development (R&D) to explore new possibilities and develop innovative products or services.

Embrace New Technologies: Stay informed about emerging technologies and explore how they can be integrated into your business operations to streamline processes or enhance the customer experience.

Embrace Collaboration: Encourage collaboration between different departments within your organization. Cross-functional teams can foster new ideas and approaches.

Celebrate Innovation: Recognize and celebrate innovative achievements within your team. This will further incentivize creative thinking and risk-taking.

CONCLUSION: THE JOURNEY TO SUCCESS IS CONTINUOUS

Mastering the modern marketplace isn't a one-time feat; it's an ongoing journey of adaptation, learning, and innovation. By embracing lifelong learning and fostering a culture of creativity within your organization, you empower your small business to thrive in the face of change. Remember, the most successful companies are unafraid to evolve, experiment, and embrace new possibilities. So, keep learning, keep innovating, and keep pushing the boundaries. The future of your business is bright!

Final Words:

We hope this comprehensive guide has equipped you with the knowledge and tools to navigate the modern marketplace and achieve long-term success. Remember, the journey to success is paved with learning, adaptation, and a relentless pursuit of excellence. The strategies outlined in this book serve as a springboard – the true power lies in your ability to implement them with passion, dedication, and a constant thirst for knowledge. With commitment and a touch of innovation, your small business can flourish and become a force to be reckoned with in the ever-evolving marketplace.

www.ingramcontent.com/pod-product-compliance
Lightning Source LLC
Chambersburg PA
CBHW050241230526
45470CB00005B/2058